CARMELA KOLMAN

Retrospective: 1982–2016

ARTIST'S STATEMENT

I was born, and remain, blind in one eye. I was visually impaired in the other. As a child, I painted constantly, with my face pressed close to the canvas. I was living in a cloud. I only painted objects that were close to me because my visual world was smaller. I would have to really look and study things to make them out. I could not recognize someone more than three feet from me. Blue eyes? I didn't know what blue eyes were. Distant views were not something that I knew — and would certainly never paint.

I'd start a drawing, often copying a photograph of a face, and stay up, reworking parts of it. I remember, at age eight, working on a nose for three hours. My mother never had a clue what I was doing all hours of the night. Then, in school the next day, I sometimes fell asleep. Teachers worried that something was wrong.

As a teenager I developed cataracts. In art school, I stood out. The assignment would be to paint a bowl, so I would — but it always looked different from everyone else's bowls. My vision was blurry, and I painted what I saw, so it came out looking very impressionistic.

I hated my faulty vision, and I hated the paintings that were produced by that vision. My beautiful blurry paintings were only blurry because that's how I saw. And everyone wanted to paint blurry like I did. I knew that if I had perfect vision, my work would look very different. I worried that if my cataracts were removed, giving me perfect vision, the work would no longer be unique. I felt like a fraud. I often threw my paintings in the garbage, only to have them dug out by well-meaning students, left by my door, a note attached: "Reconsider this."

At age 22, I was operated on for my cataracts and was given perfect vision for the first time in my life. Bugs were no longer just bugs; there were striped bees, red-dotted ladybugs, houseflies with clear wings, and some bugs even had hair. How strange. There was dirt and dust everywhere. And people didn't just have eyes; eyes were different colors, blue, brown, even gray. And their skin was a messy collage of wrinkles, scars. and hair.

At first it felt like I was watching a movie featuring someone else's vision. It was so clear that it didn't seem as though it belonged to me. It was too much for me to handle. It took me years to feel that it belonged to me — that it was mine and not someone else's. I had to relearn how to paint.

After painting fruit, I am now drawn to flowers, specifically roses. Roses interest me because they are multi-layered, have many intersecting planes, are delicate and colorful, opaque and translucent. I carve out the shapes and try to catch the flickering light on the petals. Each rose has intricate depth and many abstract shapes. I enjoy integrating the compositions with the depth of the petals, their abstract shapes, and the flatness of the picture plane.

I developed a fondness for roses because my husband planted many rose bushes at our Port Jefferson home where my studio is located. Each summer I enjoy watching them bloom with color.

Carmela Kolman, August 2016

VITALITY SEIZED

Suzaan Boettger

Clusters of softly glistening grapes, pears shimmering in darkened atmospheres, glowing peach spheres, and gleaming apples — fruits of knowledge and seduction — were the radiances that Carmela Kolman brought forth during the mid-period of her professional career. With objects isolated against fields in muted hues, these compositions offered minimalist evocations of the traditional genre she excelled at — still life. When shown after the Great Recession following the 2007 market crash, the provocative juxtapositions of sensuality and restraint spoke to conflicted desires in a period of political flux and fiscal instabilities. As the economy recovered, her small, richly hued orbs splayed across white planes played with oscillating associations of juicy pieces of fruit and Tutti-Frutti candies. But twinned to the gumdrops' brightness were shadows.

Carmela was a well-respected New York painter (RISD BFA; Yale MFA) who regularly exhibited in solo and group shows in the trendiest precincts of Manhattan art galleries and elsewhere. She actively participated in the artists' group devoted to still life painting, Zeuxis, with whom she showed her work throughout the United States. As did Italian modernist still life painter Giorgio Morandi in his judicious arrangements of faintly hued vessels, her paintings demonstrate her fine attention to spatial juxtapositions for dynamic adjacent shapes and the potency of negative spaces. Rather than the customary tabletop heterogeneity, Carmela signaled plenitude by the richness of individual objects.

Having focused for a decade on fruit, Carmela turned her attention to serpentine strings of luminous beads and close-ups of rose blossoms loosely brushed. Flowers, associated in historical visual culture with nature and transient beauty, have always been signs for the female. Carmela's extreme close-ups of bouquets present them in a scale so exaggerated that they call up — and invite — burying one's face in petals and inhaling the aroma. The jewelry continued the visual duality of vivid spheres loosely arranged and projecting from flattened grounds, making more explicit the feminine allure of the luscious globules. Both subjects summon sensations of abundance, fertility, and glamour.

A phase of her compositions' compressed recession and expansive space abstract the tabletop arrangements into modernist fields dotted with color. The orbs of fruit and circles of beads are often seen against ambiguous grounds that are neither table nor wall — in effect, presenting a modernist flattening of space against which they visually project. Often she subverted the traditional frontal perspective onto tabletop arrangements — the cornerstone of traditional still life — by viewing her objects from immediately above. The hovering aerial viewpoint generates an intimate proximity to the arrays.

Sometimes these grounds are in a subtly grayed or toned hue, both spatially and emotionally recessive. More frequently, contradicting the vivacity of individual objects modeled in illusionistic volumes, are cast shadows so prominently shaped and strongly colored that their presence becomes a crucial compositional element and determinant of the images' affect. The mood becomes deliberate vivaciousness against a ground of melancholy.

Carmela's pictures evoke a fervent *joie de vivre*, the desire to seize light — to literally "take pleasure" from the act of grasping and portraying its illumination of beautiful natural objects and organic forms. Of course these were in part responses to her delayed acquisition of clear sight, albeit in only one eye, at age 23. And the shadows conjure her congenital, always looming, Marfan syndrome. Her passion for pictorial brightness to forestall the fall of darkness displays her energy, fortitude, and hope. Together these elements made her, and her paintings, admirable and memorable. Carmela's images are vital *because* she knew darkness, and her striking fusions arouse attention, reflection, and gratitude for their encompassing beauty.

Suzaan Boettger, an art historian, critic, author and lecturer in New York City, and Carmela first met when Dr. Boettger selected Carmela's work for inclusion in the exhibition she guest curated for the Trabia Gallery, SoHo, on view in February 1990, "Radiant Fruit: Iconic Still Life."

PEARS

It is only initially that the subject of Carmela Kolman's new paintings appears to be pears. They are the sole object she depicts, and as fruit, are related to the abundant conglomerations of produce, flowers, fowl, and tabletop symbols of Baroque still life painting. But her arrays of pears in a single layer across the pictorial field, in loose scatters verging on a modernist grid, set aside the domestic locale and faux candidness of the traditional motif. Kolman's reductive compositions give us generic pears in slightly blurred contours and deeply saturated colors, juxtaposed to almost equally prominent darkly hued shapes between their masses.

Thus, in Kolman's hands, the substantial shadows cast by her nominal subject are fully integrated into the picture. The emotionally heightened effect can be appreciated both as dramatic abstraction and dramatized metaphor. The shape of the pears is roughly akin to that of human silhouettes. They are not upright but prone, suggesting bodies at rest, as if in darkened bedrooms variously illuminated between curtain openings at high noon, sunset, or by moonlight.

In this meditation on stilled life, the strong presence of the shadows effectively updates the genre's traditional memento mori allusions to mortality — an hourglass trickling sand from potential to past, a just-extinguished candle emitting a smoky plume, and the foreboding skull. In Kolman's intense focus on pears, her subject becomes the shifting fulcrum between this succulent sign of life and its dark side. Her images are both visually compelling and rarer still, emotionally complex.

Statement for the exhibition catalogue, *Carmela Kolman, Paintings*, Prince Street Gallery, March 2001 by Suzaan Boettger

BIOGRAPHICAL NOTE

There are a few other things you need to know to understand my sister's life and accomplishments. Carmela was born with Marfan's syndrome, a genetic connective tissue disorder that affects the eyes, the heart, and other parts of the body. After her vision was corrected in 1983, she stopped painting for several years. She got a second master's degree in social work and worked as a caseworker in Maryland and Connecticut.

In 1993, her aorta dissected. She managed to call 911 before collapsing, but if she hadn't lived a few minutes from the Yale/New Haven Medical Center, she would have died that day. After she recovered, she decided to try painting again and spent the next two decades exploring how light affected fruit and other objects.

In 2012, her aorta dissected again, requiring two additional traumatic surgeries. In the time between these two operations, she began painting roses. She created more than two dozen paintings in a few months, working despite constant pain.

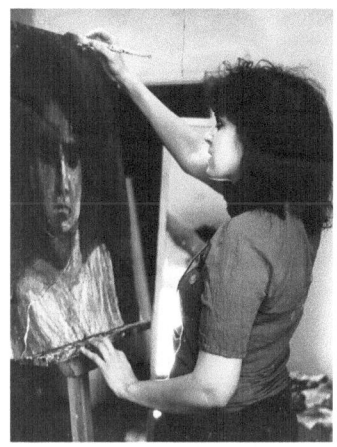

Carmela Kolman at age 20

In March 2018, her doctors told her she needed a fourth surgery to repair the rest of her aorta. Although the operation was successful, she died a few days later from an arrhythmia that was impossible to predict or prevent and that often affects people who have had multiple surgeries.

When we say somebody is gifted, we are really talking about a genetic gift. When nature gave Carmela her genetic package, it threw in remarkable artistic talent, as if to make up for the deficiencies in the rest of the order. You'll see what she did with that talent in the pages that follow.

Joe Kolman, April 2018

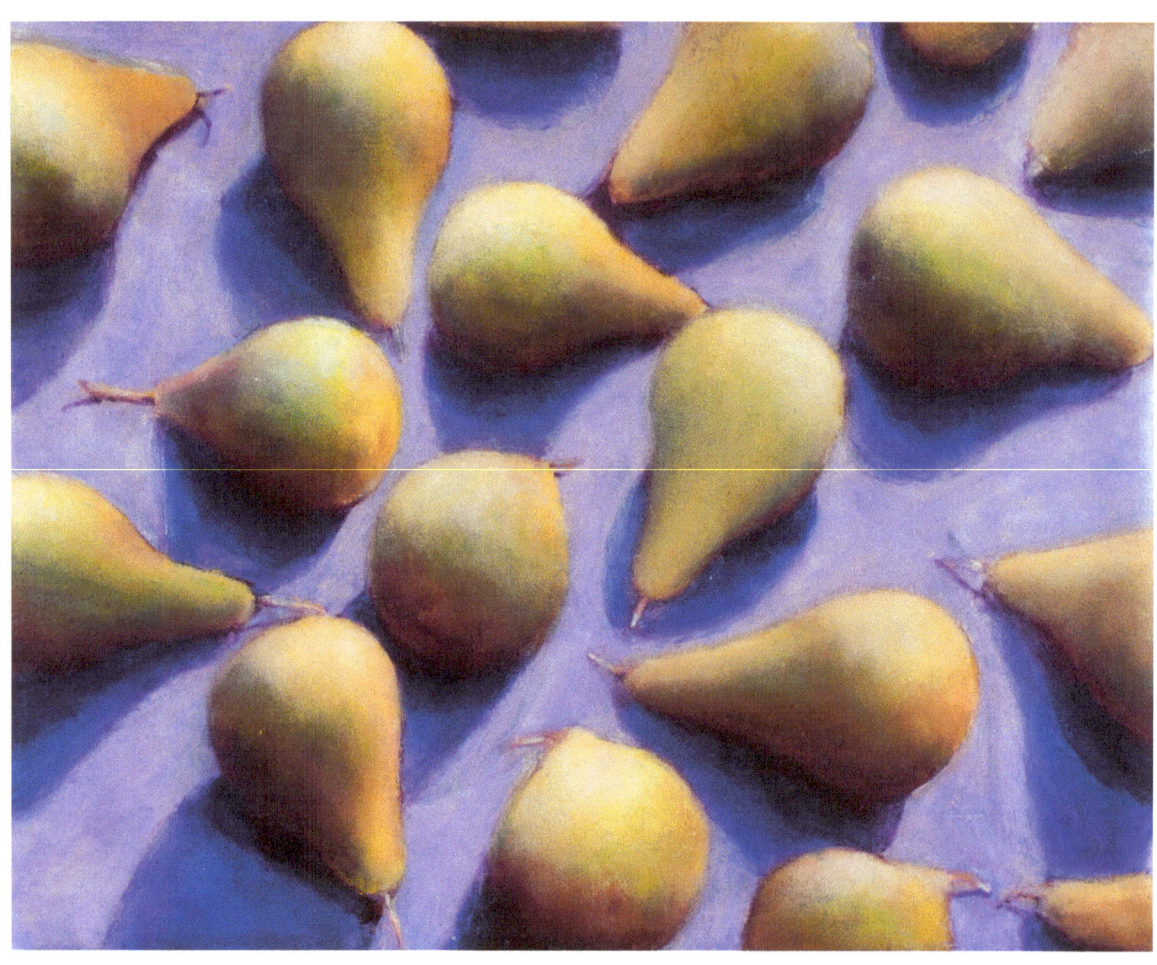

Blue Pears
20 x 26 in

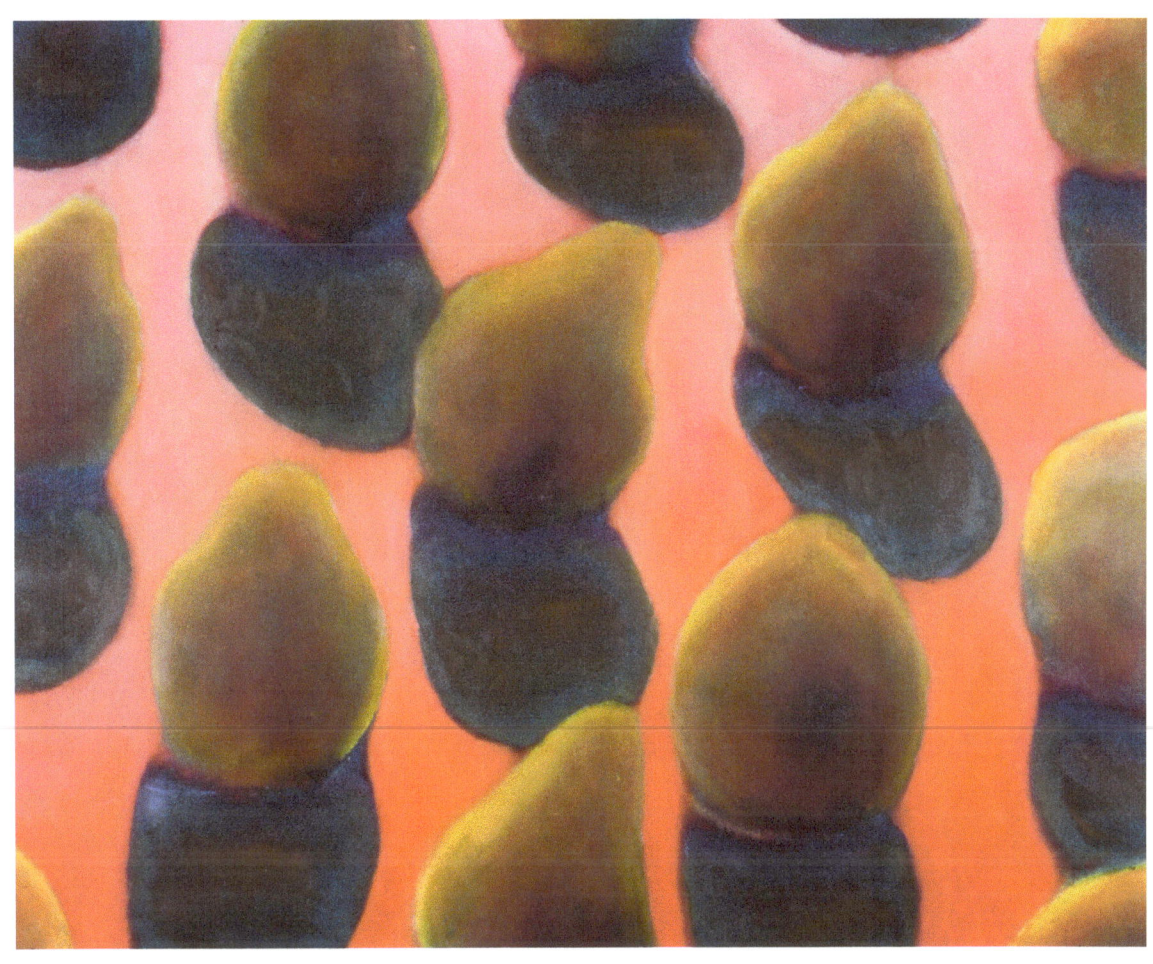

South Beach Pears
20 x 26 in

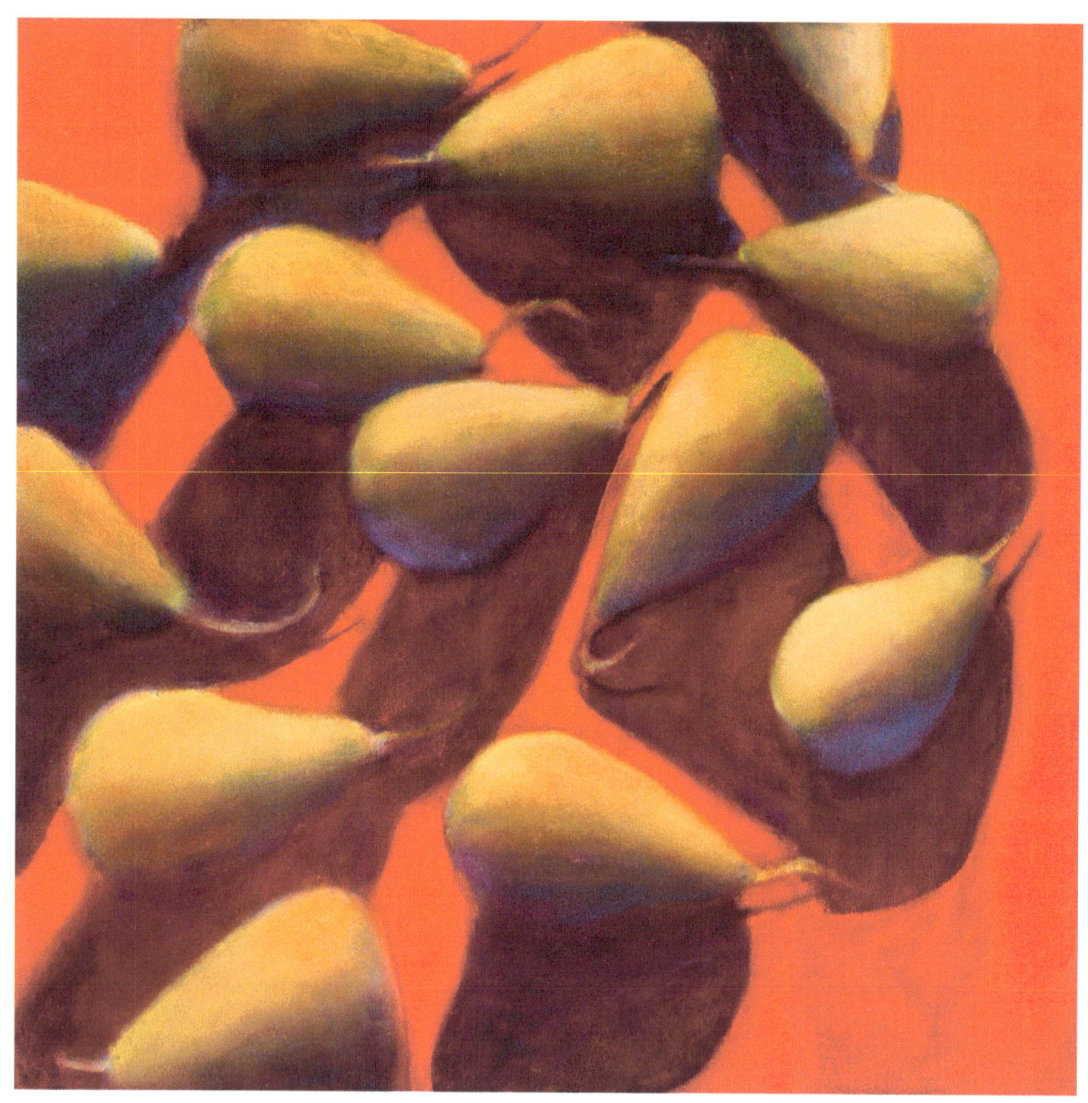

Stolen Pears
30 x 36 in

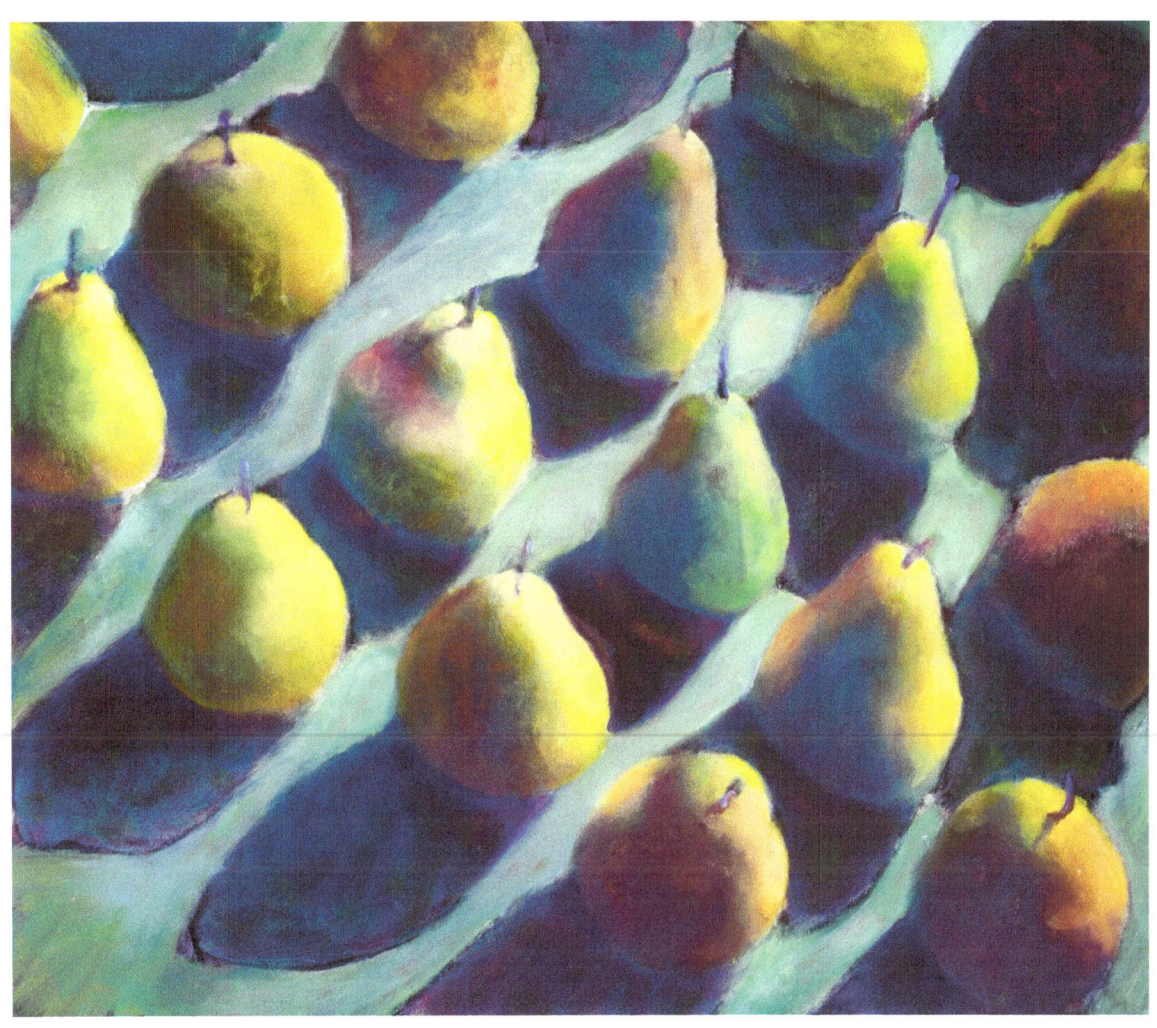

Militant Pears
30 x 36 in

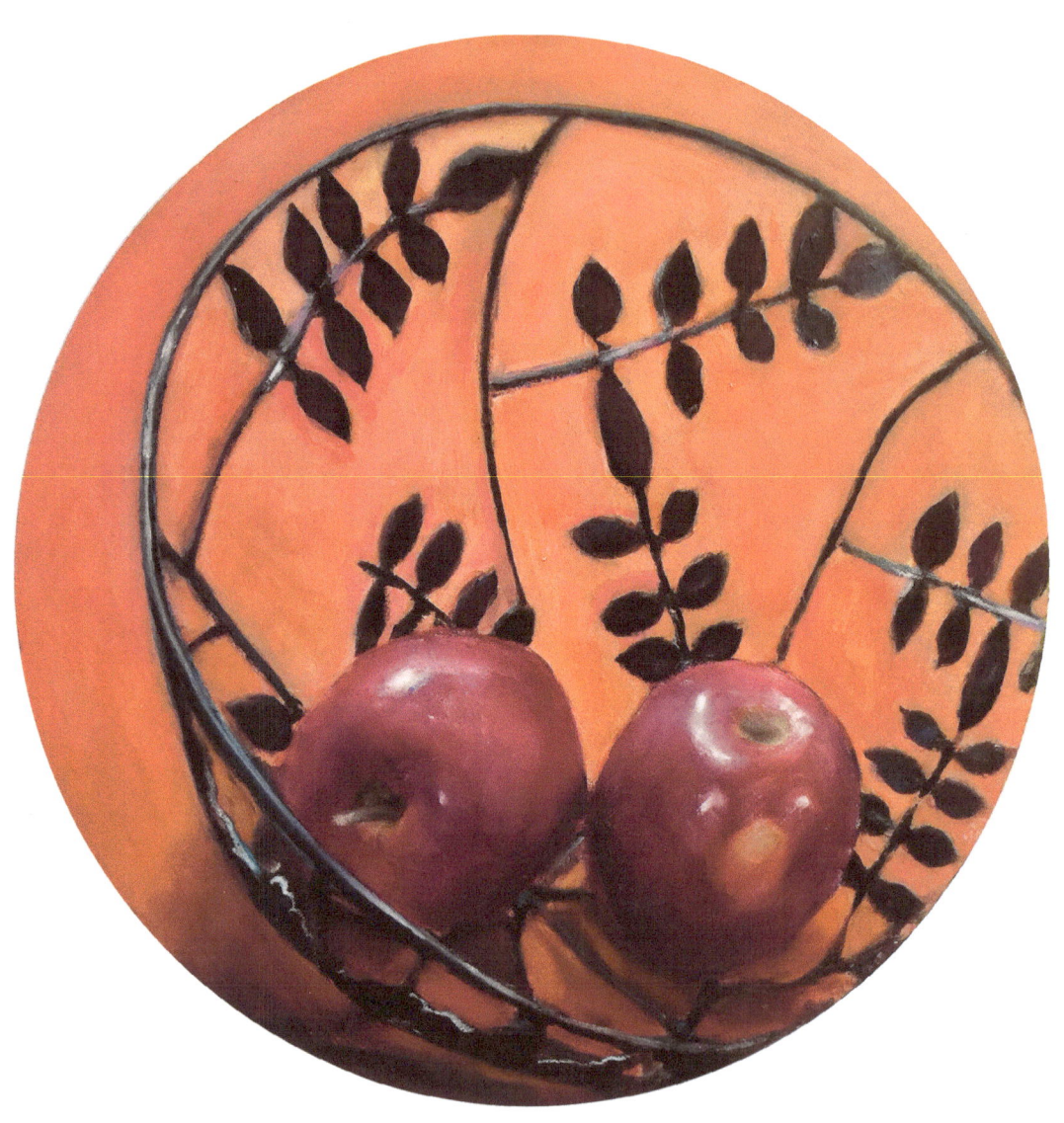

Apples in Wire Basket
20 x 20 in

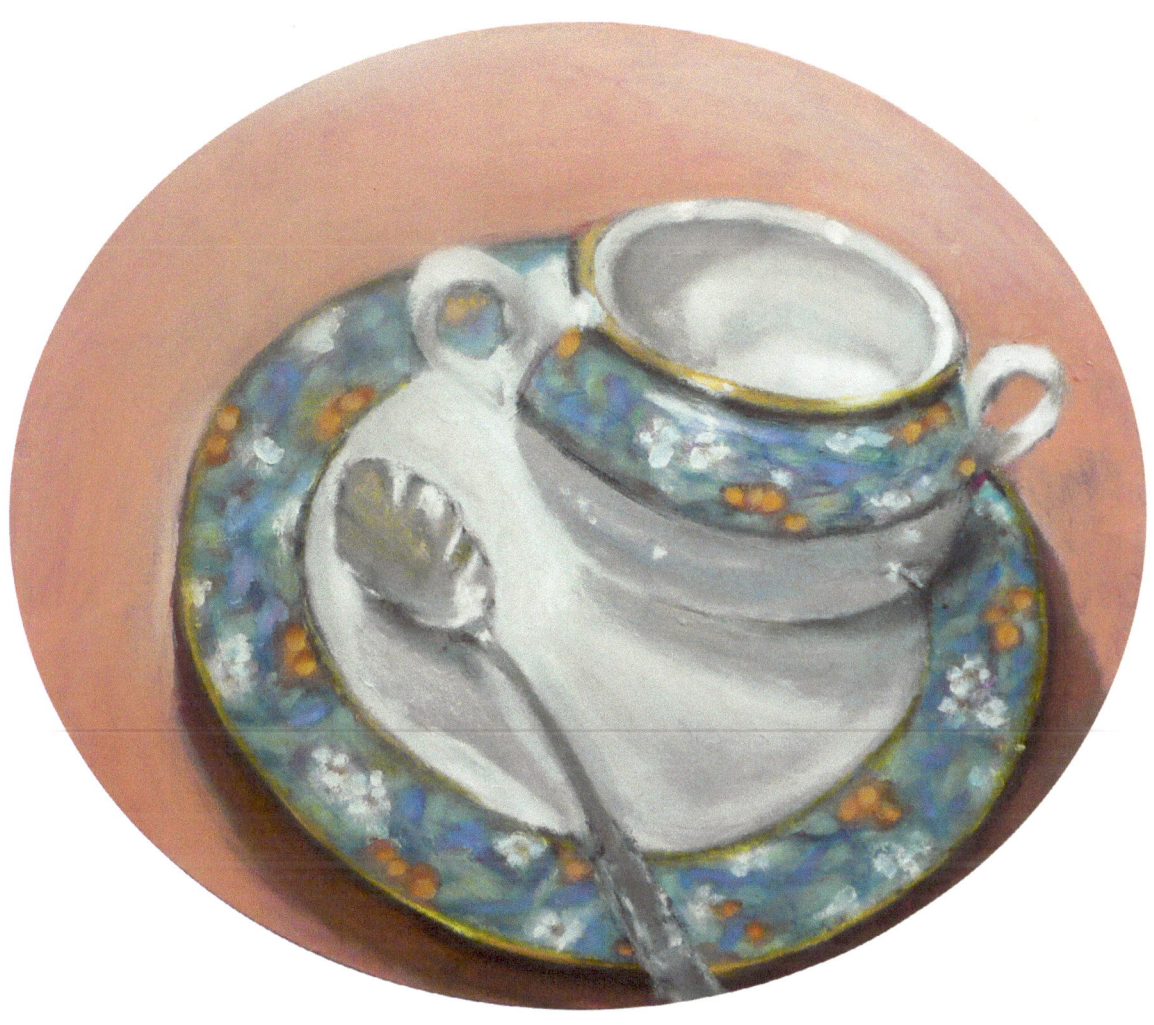

Sugar Bowl
20 x 24 in

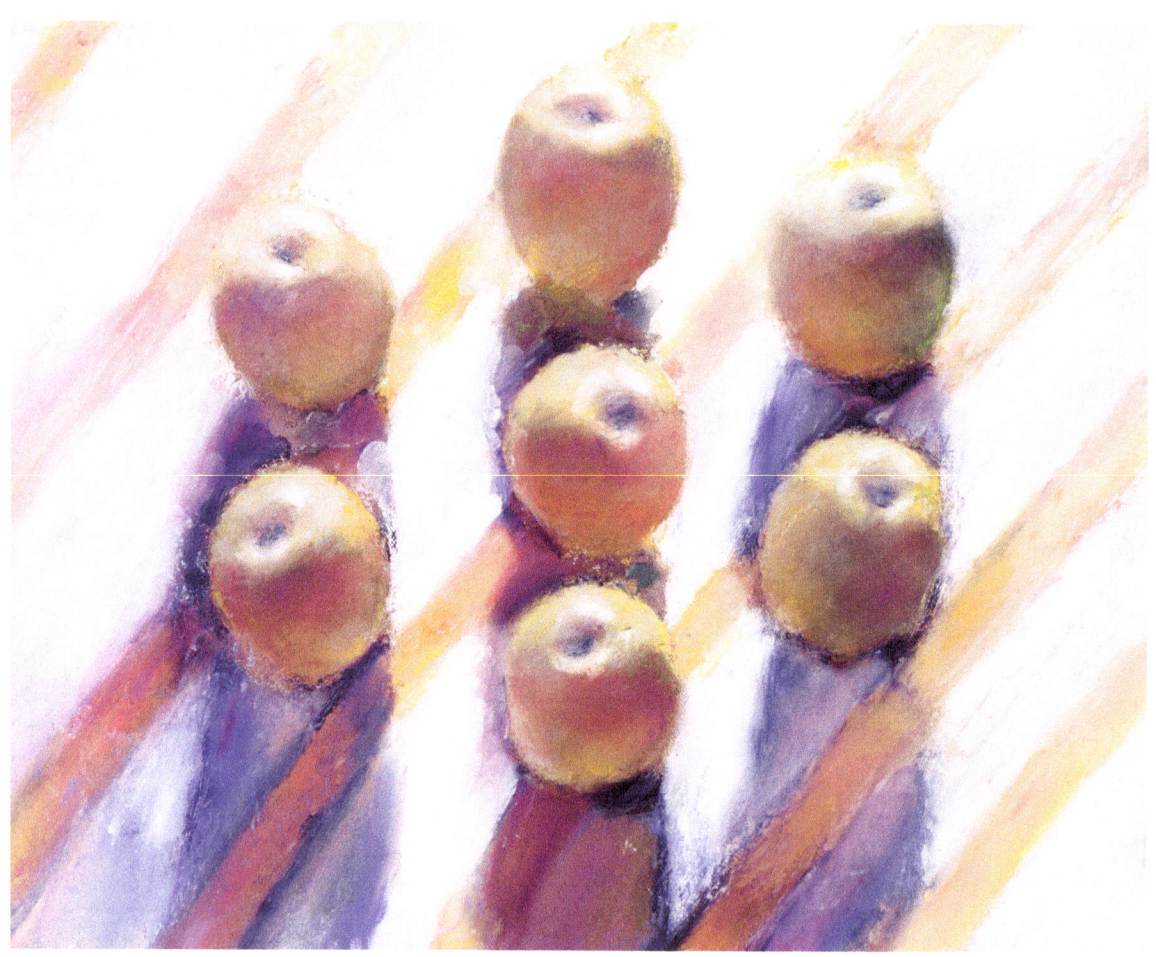

Seven Apples
15 x 18 in

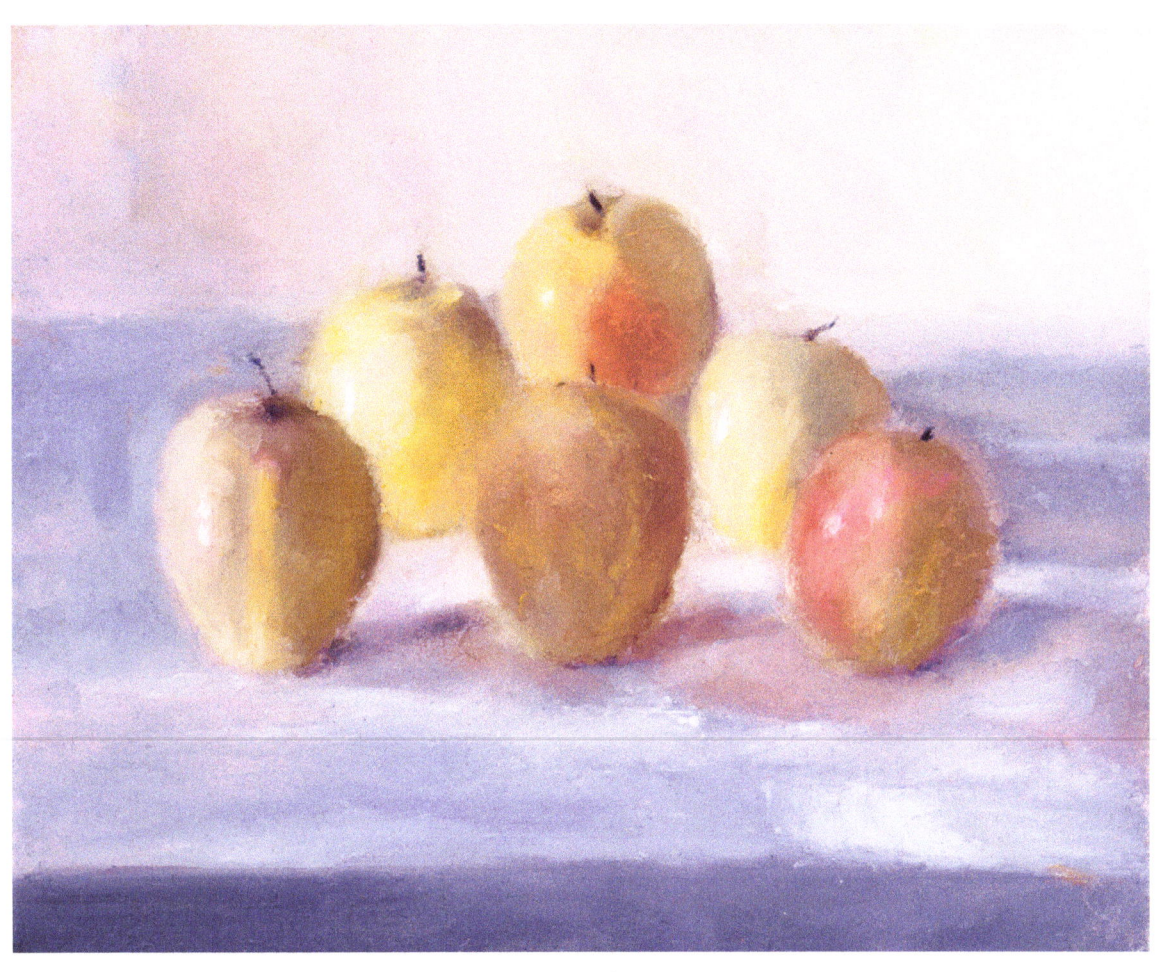

Bowling Anyone?
14 x 17 in

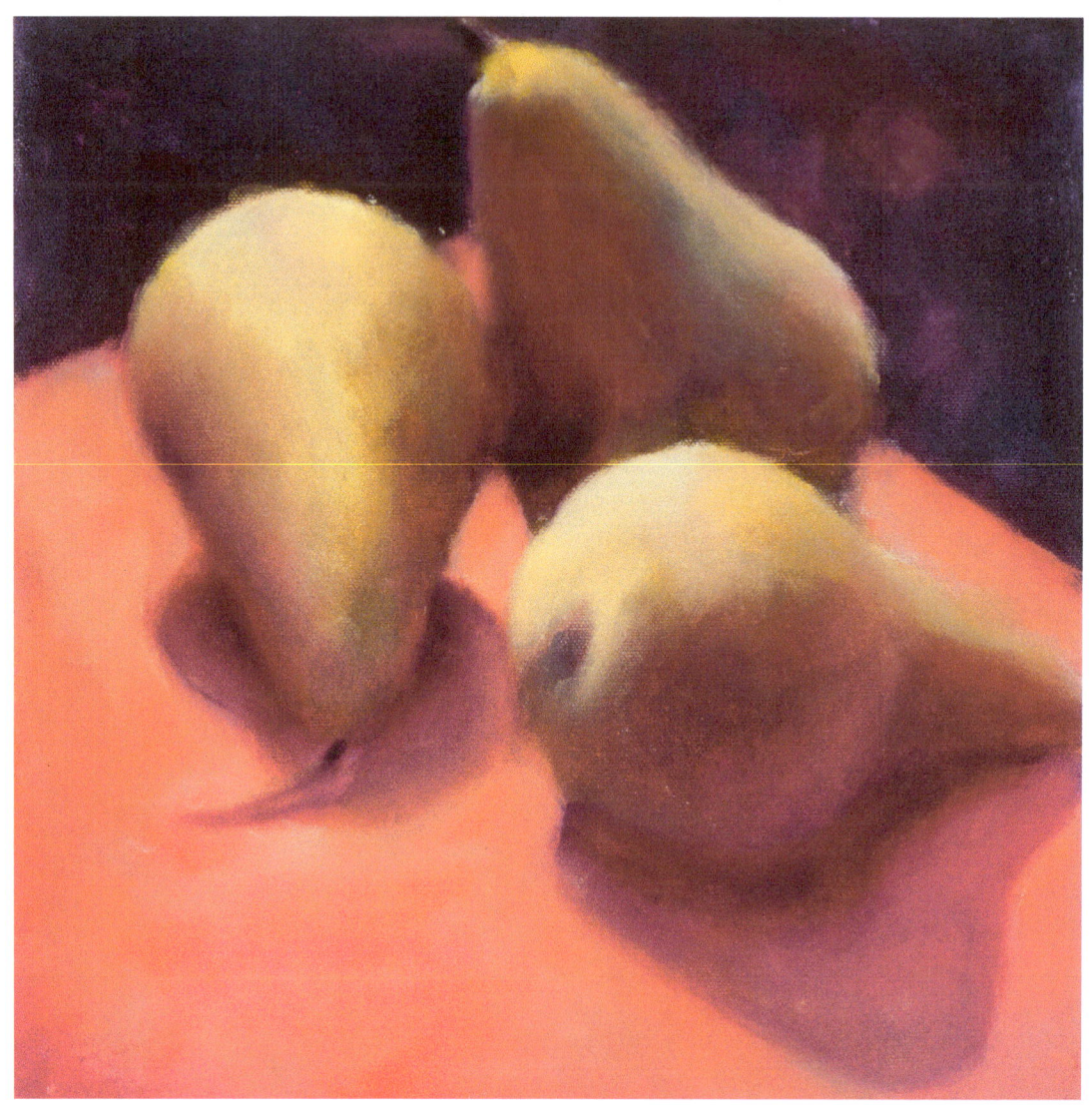

Three Pears on Pink Cloth
16 x 16 in

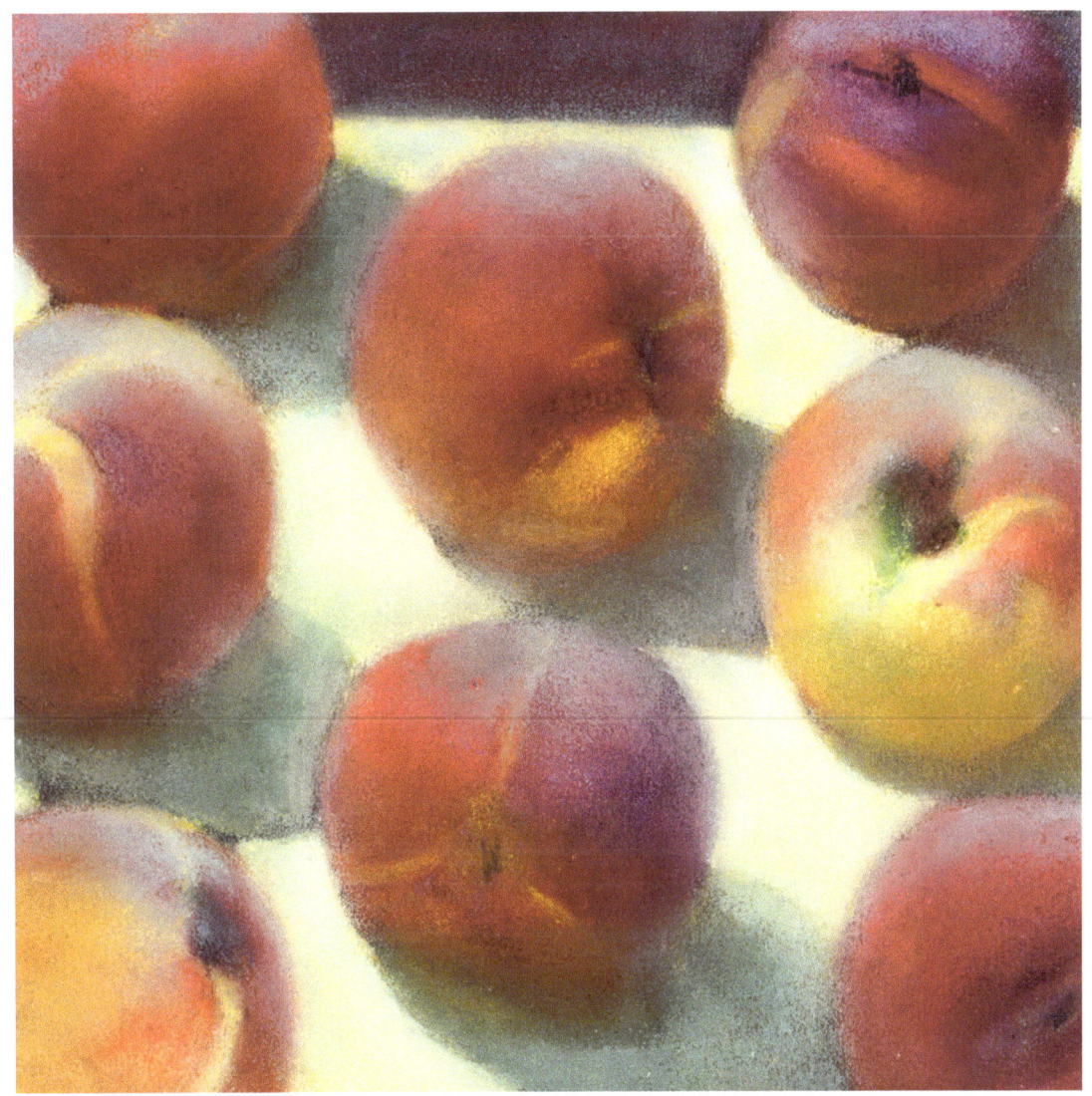

Eight Peaches
16 x 16 in

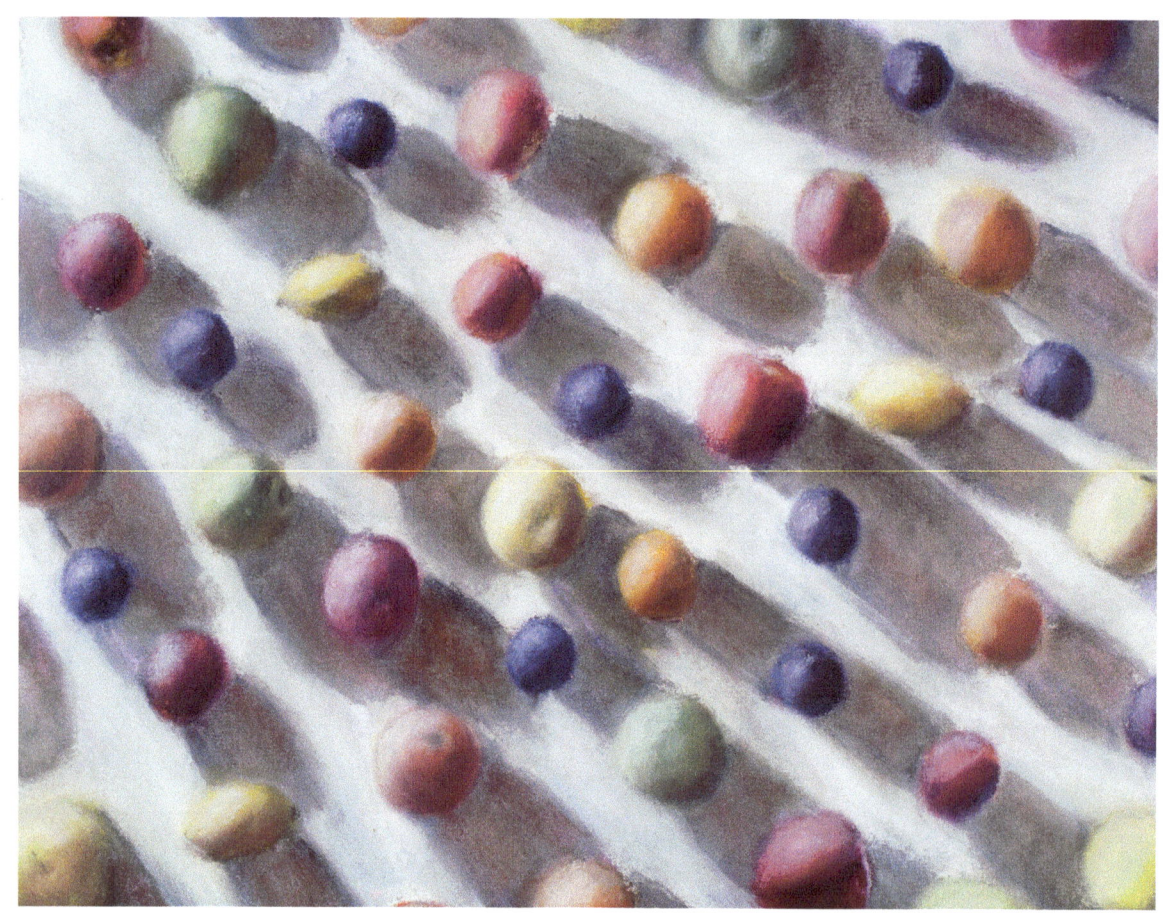

Mixed Fruit
20 x 26 in

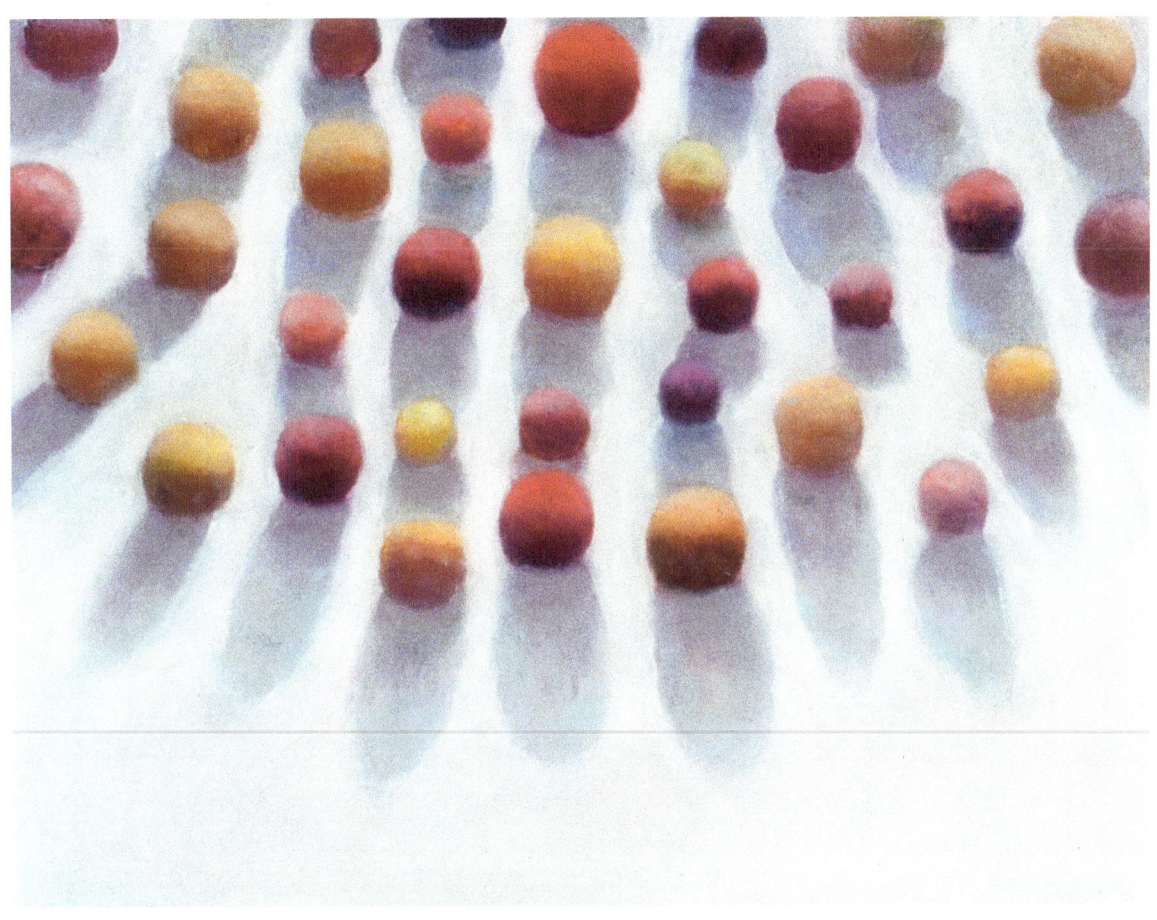

Invasion
20 x 26 in

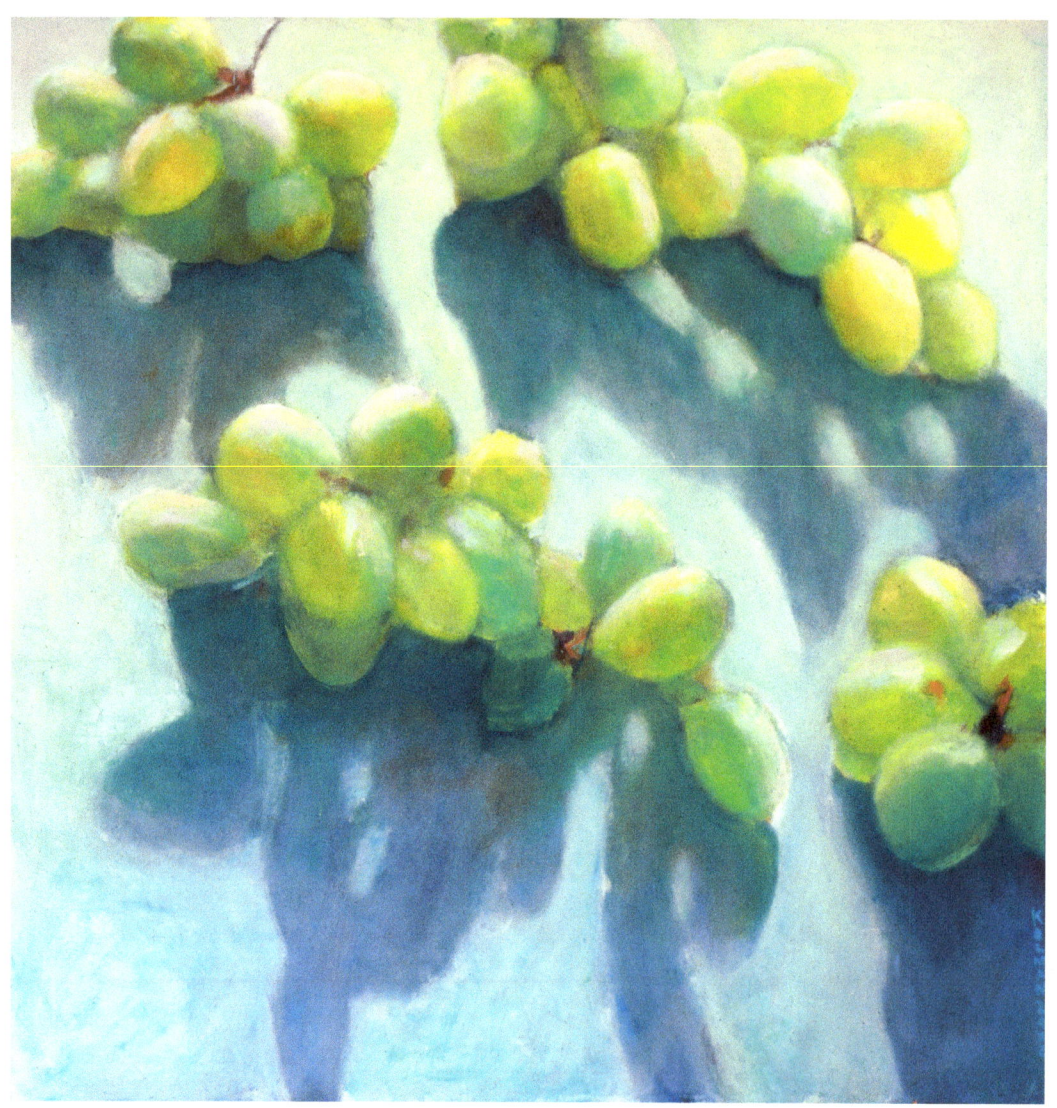

Green Grapes
40 x 48 in

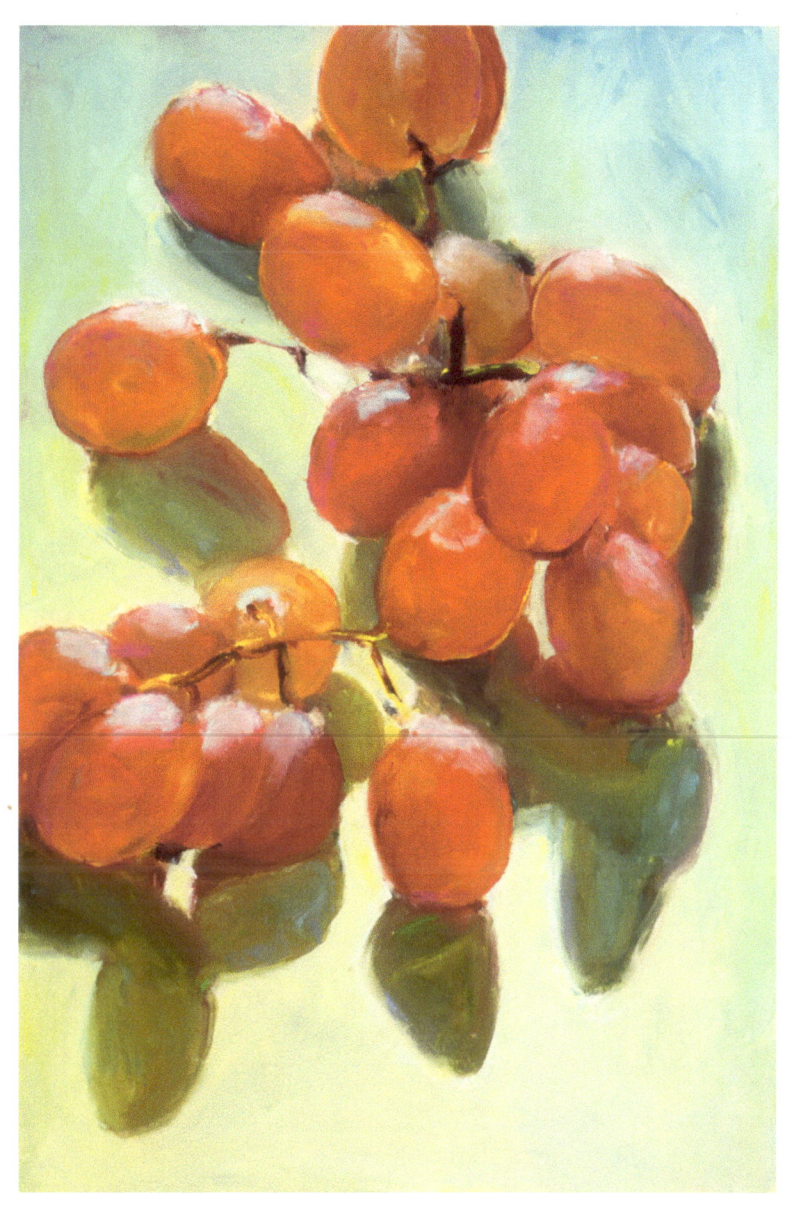

Sparkling Grapes
36 x 24 in

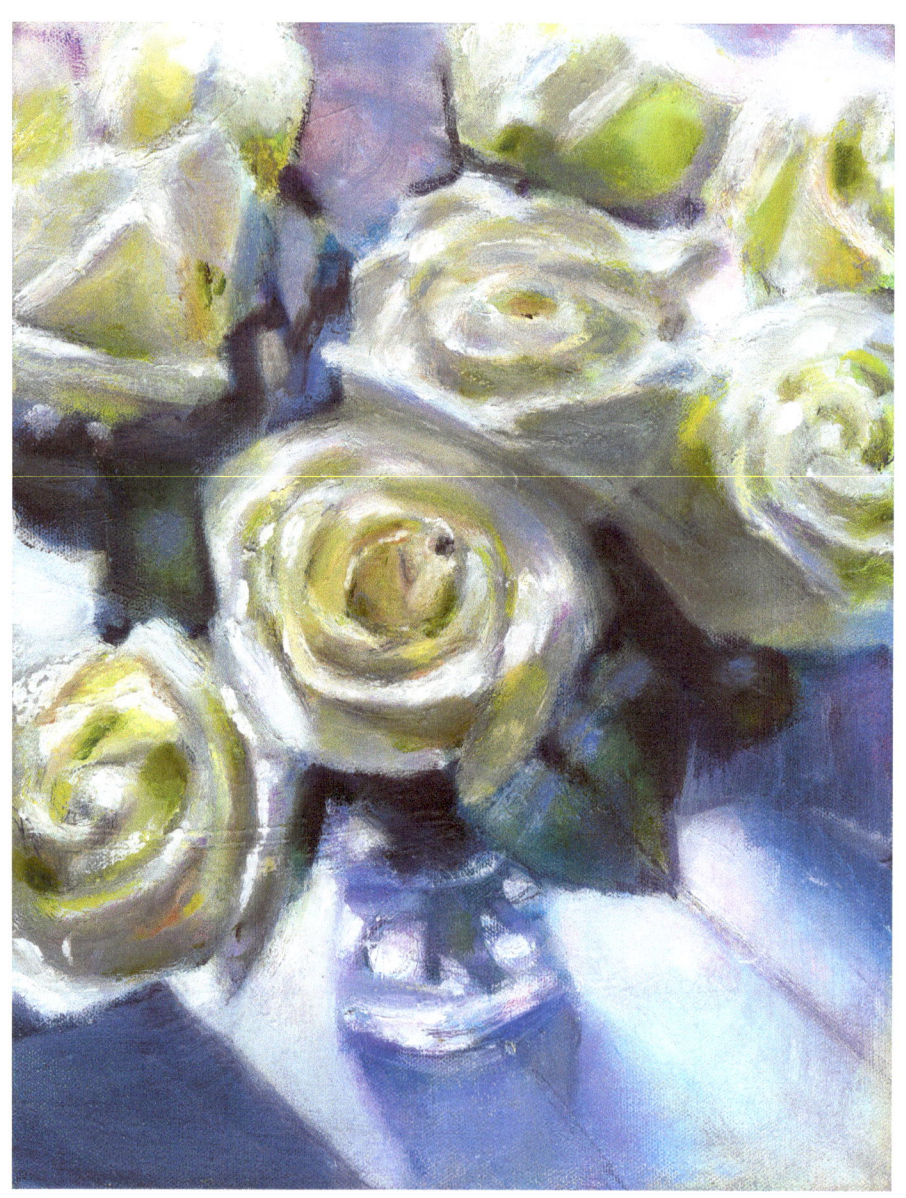

Sunlit Roses
14 x 11 in

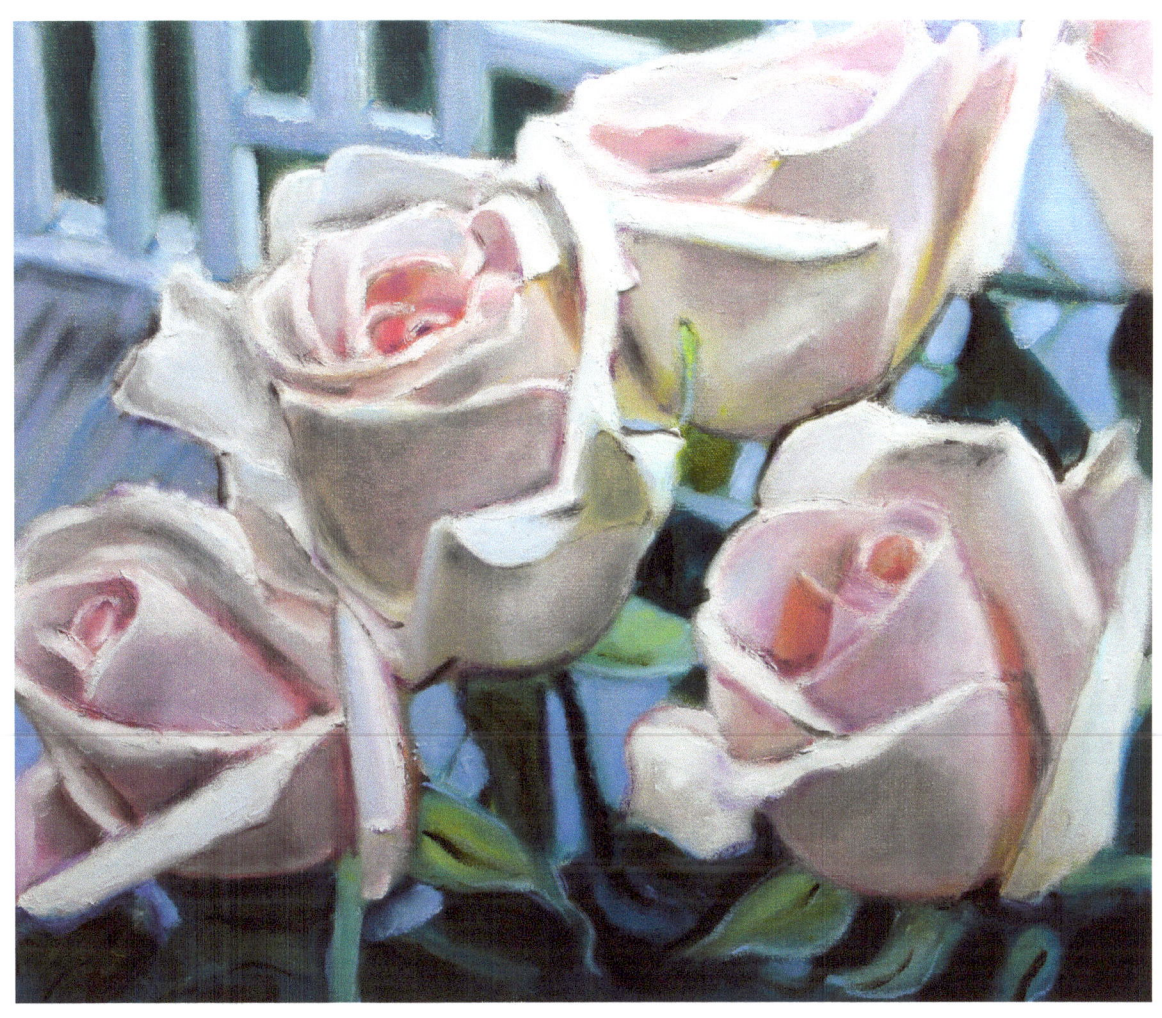

On the Porch
20 x 24 in

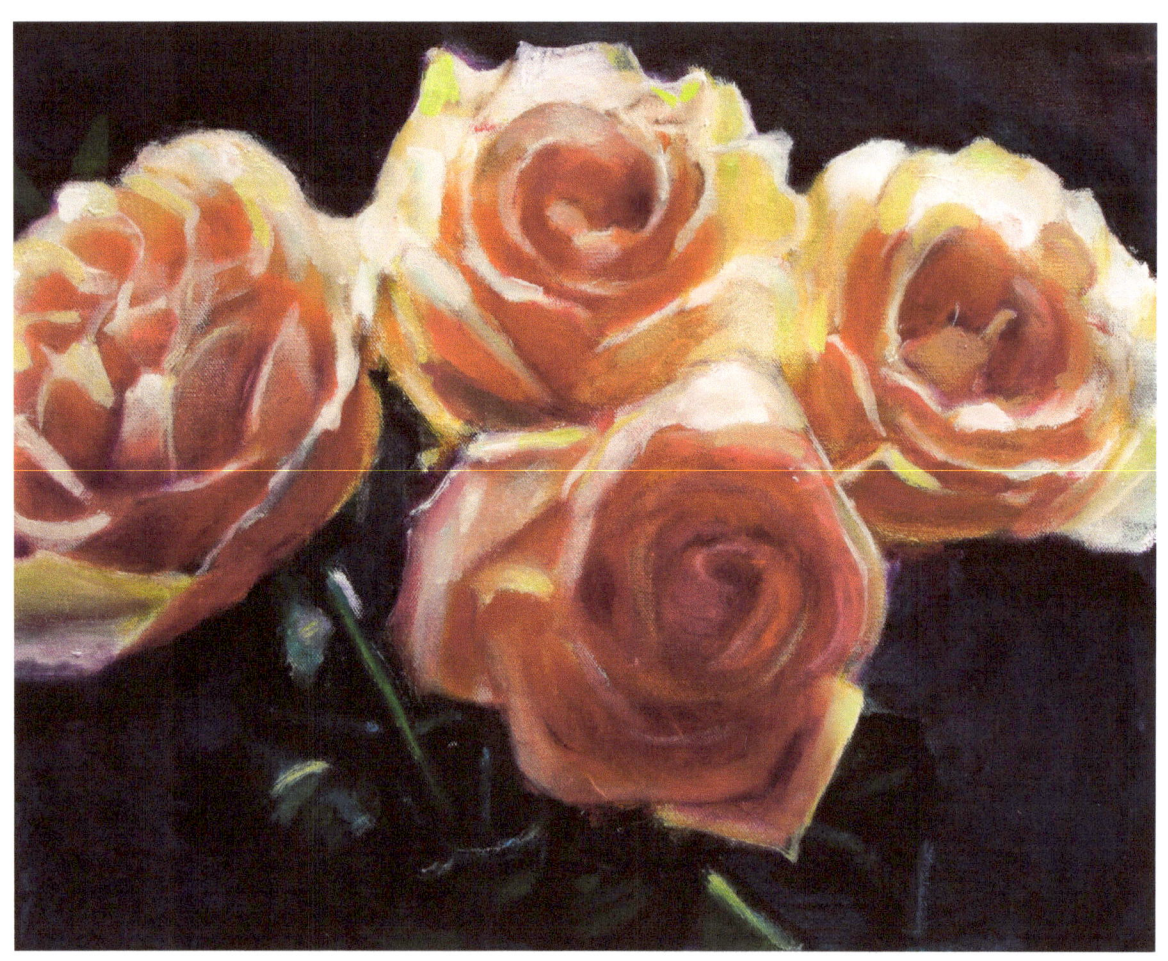

Four Roses
16 x 24 in

CURRICULUM VITAE

EDUCATION
1984   MFA, Yale University School of Art, New Haven, CT
1982   BFA, Rhode Island School of Design, Providence, RI

SOLO AND TWO-PERSON EXHIBITIONS
2015   The Painting Center, New York, NY
2013   Art Access Gallery, Columbus, OH
2012   The Painting Center, New York, NY
2008   The Painting Center, New York, NY
2007   The Painting Center, New York, NY
2005   Art Access Gallery, Columbus, OH
2003   LaGuardia College, Long Island City
2002   Art Access Gallery, Columbus, OH
2002   Denise Bibro Gallery, New York, NY
2001   Prince Street Gallery, New York, NY
2001   Art Access Gallery, Columbus, OH
2000   Prince Street Gallery, New York, NY
2000   Clark House Gallery, Bangor, ME
1998   Randall Tuttle Fine Arts, Woodbury, CT
1996   Erector Square Gallery, New Haven, CT
1996   T.A.I. Gallery, New York, NY
1995   Erector Square Gallery, New Haven, CT
1995   John Slade Ely House, New Haven, CT
1984   Yale School of Art Gallery, New Haven, CT

SELECTED GROUP EXHIBITIONS
2012-13   Traveling Exhibition: Reflections, Zeuxis: Lindenwood University, St. Charles, MO; Southeast Missouri State University, Cape Girardeau; Coe College, Cedar Rapids, IA; The Painting Center, New York, NY; Pennsylvania College of Art and Design, Lancaster
2010-12   Traveling Exhibition: The Common Object, Zeuxis: Lancaster Museum of Art, Lancaster, PA; Peninsula Fine Arts Center, Newport News, VA; Prince Street Gallery, New York, NY; MICA, Baltimore, MD
2009   Broome Street Gallery, New York, NY, Zeuxis In/Out
2008   Hobart and William Smith Colleges, Geneva, NY, Zeuxis In/Out
2008   First Street Gallery, New York, NY, Zeuxis: Small Takes
2008   Central Gallery, Old Saybrook, CT, Feast for the Eyes
2007-09   Gallery North, Stony Brook, CT
2007   Omni Gallery, Uniondale, NY, Evocative Space of the Familiar
2006   Bendheim Gallery, Greenwich, CT, The Persistance of Paint
2006-07   Traveling Exhibition: Facets of Perception, Zeuxis: Notre Dame de Namur University, Belmont, CA; Snug Harbor Cultural Center, Staten Island, NY; Schweinfurth Memorial Art Center, Auburn, NY; Hollins University, Roanoke, VA; University of Tulsa, OK; The College of William & Mary, Williamsburg, VA
2004   The Painter's Touch, Gallery North, Stony Brook, NY, New Visions
2004   Neptune Gallery, New York, NY, Spring Exhibition
2004-05   Traveling Exhibition: Tabletop Arenas, Zeuxis: Lori Bookstein Gallery, New York, NY; University of New Hampshire, Dover; Colby College Museum of Art, Waterville, ME; Haverford College, Haverford, PA; Ohr-O'Keefe Museum of Art, Biloxi, MS

2003	Westbeth Gallery, New York, NY, Zeuxis, A Moveable Feast
2003	Salena Gallery, Long Island University, Brookville, NY, Zeuxis
2003	Omni Gallery, Uniondale, NY, Objects of Interest
2002	Attleoboro Museum, Attleboro, MA, Zeuxis, Still Life and Small Works 2
2002	Denise Bibro Fine Art, New York, NY, Summer Exhibition
2002	Traveling Exhibition: Uncommon Perspectives, 2002: Denise Bibro Fine Art, New York, NY; Hermitage Foundation Museum, Norfolk, VA
2002	Washington Art Association, Washington Depot, CT
2001-02	Traveling Exhibition: Zeuxis, Serial Thinking: Wright State University, Dayton, OH; Kouros Gallery, New York, NY; Augustana College, Rock Island, IL; Purdue University, West Lafayette, IN
2000	College of William and Mary, Williamsburg, VA, Zeuxis
2000	Olson-Larsen Gallery, West Des Moines, IA, Zeuxis
2000	Boston International Fine Art Show (with Clark House Gallery), MA
1999	Traveling Exhibition: Zeuxis, The Human Presence: University of Wisconsin-La Crosse; Peninsula Fine Arts Center, Newport News, VA; The Washington Studio School, Washington, DC; Erector Square Gallery, New Haven, CT; The Painting Center, New York, NY
1999	Erector Square Gallery, New Haven, CT, Contemporary Painting, Andrew Forge, Juror, Award recipient
1999	Prince Street Gallery, New York, NY, Distilled Life
1999	Marywood University, Scranton, PA, Zeuxis at Marywood
1999	Marymount College, Tarrytown, NY, Zeuxis, An Association of Still Life Painters
1998	Boston University, Sherman Gallery, MA, Small Works
1998	Erector Square Gallery, New Haven, Connecticut Commission on the Arts, Exhibition of Fellowship Recipients
1998	Connecticut Commission on the Arts, Hartford, Exhibition of Fellowship Recipients

BIBLIOGRAPHY

New York Daily News, Nov. 15, 2012. Article. Clem Richardson.
Zeuxis catalog, 2010. Review. Imagen Sara Smith.
Better Homes and Gardens, Jul./Aug. 2005. Featured Artist.
Zeuxis catalog, 2004. Review. Thomas M. Disch.
Long Island Press, Sept. 2004. Review. Deborah Wolfe.
Boston Globe, Sept. 5, 2004. Photo Reproduction.
Atlantic News, Aug. 26, 2004. Photo Reproduction.
Wolf Moon Press Journal, July 2004. Review. Laurie Meunier Graves.
Art New England, Aug./Sept. 2003. Photo Reproduction. Rich McKown.
The New York Times, May 11, 2003. Review. Helen A. Harrison.
The New York Daily News, Feb. 9, 2003. Joe Dziemianowicz.
Columbus Dispatch, Nov. 17, 2002. Review. Jacqueline Hall.
Modern Painters, Spring 2001. Karen Wright. Photo Reproduction. Gallery.
New York Daily News, March 2001. Photo Reproduction. Today in New York.
Where Magazine, March 2001. Photo Reproduction. Art and Antiques Guide
Columbus Dispatch, Aug. 12, 2001. Review. Jacqueline Hall.
Hartford Advocate, Jan. 14, 1999. Review. Patricia Rosoff.
Rockville Journal Inquirer, Dec. 25, 1998. Review. Steve Starger.
New Haven Advocate, Dec. 17, 1998. Review. Willoughby Mariano.
New Haven Register, Dec. 13, 1998. Review. Judy Birke.
Waterbury Republican, June 28, 1998. Review. Tracy O'Shaughnessy.
New Haven Register, Jan. 1998. Review. Karen Singer.
New Haven Register, Jan. 1995. Review. Judy Birke.

AWARDS

1999	Juror's Award, Contemporary Painting, Erector Square Gallery, New Haven, CT. Juror: Andrew Forge
1998	The Connecticut Commission on the Arts, Fellowship
1979, '84	The Gore Foundation, Full Scholarship for undergraduate and graduate education

www.ingramcontent.com/pod-product-compliance
Lightning Source LLC
Chambersburg PA
CBHW051831210526
45473CB00005B/1833